(the story / formula)™

KELLY SWANSON

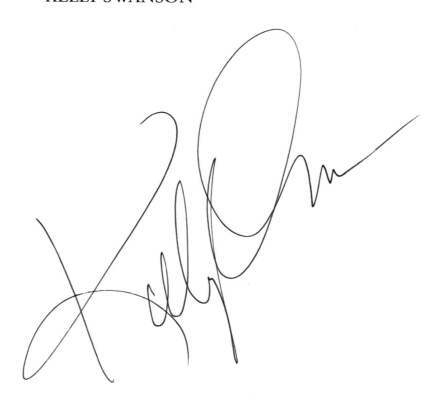

(*dedication*)

This book is dedicated to Bill and Will, for their never-ending patience and support, and for all the hours they had to listen to Mom rattle on about stories. I love you both more than I ever say.

This book is also dedicated to Laurie Guest who, unlike my family, didn't have to listen, and did anyway. There will always be a seat beside me for you, my friend.

This book is also dedicated to my new friend, Dave Bricker who is without question the true brain behind this book's layout. Thank you, Dave, for your tireless devotion to the way I share my story.

(*foreword*)
—————————
by Dave Bricker

THE EXTRAORDINARY PRINCESS

Once upon a time in a not-so-faraway kingdom there lived an extraordinary little princess. She was not the kingdom's prettiest little girl, nor could she run the fastest, hold her breath the longest, or—though she might have bragged otherwise—eat the most pies at the county fair. Truth be told, the king and queen were not her parents; they didn't even know her name. She was extraordinary because all little girls and boys are extraordinary—each in their own way—and she was a princess because every little girl is a princess.

When the extraordinary little princess was growing up, she didn't know she was extraordinary. In fact, because she was one of those children who never worried about being first in line and always seemed to be dancing to music no one else could hear (and who occasionally ate too much pie but never quite enough to win a prize), she was led to believe she was anything *but* extraordinary.

But the princess didn't worry about what the other children thought. What they didn't know was that not only could she dance to music they couldn't hear, she could see an entire kingdom they couldn't see—a town full of extraordinary ordinary people: the baker and the schoolteacher, the bishop and the court jester, knights and maids in waiting, farmers, drunkards, mischievous children, shop owners, a doctor, an old sea captain, and even an extraordinary ordinary king and queen with a daughter of their own.

And though the extraordinary princess could see everybody in this kingdom that no one else could see, nobody who lived there could see her. She had great affection for the people there, and because in that world, she was both magical and invisible, she busied herself with the task of making sure their lives were always meaningful. There was the day the farmer ploughed up a golden key she had hidden in his field. Another day, the town drunk found out he was the king's cousin because the princess sent him a mysterious letter. (They never did figure out where that came from). And there was the time that salesman came to town selling all sorts of fancy cures and potions—until the princess slipped him a piece of pie that was a few too many days south of fresh and he had to call upon the king's doctor and confess that most of his own medicines were still "under development." And then there was the time … well … maybe it's best to skip the story about the bishop.

The extraordinary princess lived a rather ordinary life and grew as children do. And though she had never promised to keep her invisible kingdom a secret, she knew her classmates might not be so accepting of what they could not see. They already wondered why she'd smile at the oddest times—and why she'd occasionally burst into giggles for no apparent reason.

One day in school, the extraordinary princess was asked by her teacher to tell a story. She stood up, walked obediently to the front of the schoolhouse, and began to recite. It didn't dawn on her until after she'd introduced the blacksmith and what almost turned out to be a real treasure map that her secret world was no longer secret, but what could she do? She finished her story, smiled politely, and looked down shyly at the floor in front of her.

What happened next was unexpected—in fact, it was extraordinary. Everyone in the classroom, including the teacher, stood up and clapped and cheered. A few of them dabbed their eyes with handkerchiefs. At that moment, the extraordinary princess became a *storyteller*—one who told stories about extraordinary ordinary people from an extraordinary ordinary place.

Word spread quickly about the extraordinary princess's gift. Soon she was telling stories about extraordinary ordinary people at fairs and parties and festivals. She told stories about extraordinary ordinary people to extraordinary ordinary farmers and bankers and doctors and merchants. She even told stories about extraordinary ordinary people to the king and his court. The extraordinary princess had great affection for the people who listened to her stories, and she busied herself with the task of making sure their lives were always meaningful. They came away feeling that their lives were perhaps a little richer than they'd thought. They felt better about themselves. They went on about their daily business with a smile and a lightness to their step.

People began to understand that storytelling was powerful magic. One day, they asked the extraordinary princess to teach them how to tell their stories. "Where do you get your magic?" they asked. "Do you use a special recipe?" "How can I tell the story of my flour mill?" "How can I tell the story of my fresh hot cakes?" "What story should I write on the sign in front of my shop?"

The extraordinary princess thought long and hard about how to teach storytelling. She had never used a recipe or a spell. She had never relied on a method or a list of ingredients. What the people were asking for came naturally to her. There was nothing extraordinary about it. Teaching *how* to tell stories felt like teaching *how* to breathe or *how* to walk down the road without floating up into the sky. She thought about the stories she told about the kingdom only she could see. They weren't so different than the "real" stories that came from the kingdom she lived in. All she'd ever done was busy herself with the task of making sure the lives of the people in *both* kingdoms were always meaningful.

And she knew that was all there was to it: Powerful stories are all about making life meaningful for ordinary extraordinary people.

She also knew that answer was too simple. As true as it was, to be meaningful itself, to abide by its own rule, it had to be wrapped in a story—a story about people with messages, ideas, and aspirations who want to communicate more deeply, motivate others, win the loyalty of clients and colleagues, and succeed at life and business. She'd break it down, make them think, make them feel, talk about finding the extraordinary in the ordinary, encourage them to focus on bettering other people's lives, explain why that would help their businesses thrive, and lead them to the simple power she knew lay at the heart of her magic.

"And I know just what I'll call this new story," said the extraordinary princess aloud to herself—"*The Story Formula.*"

Dave Bricker is a speaker, author, editor, book designer, and publishing coach who helps remarkable people tell remarkable stories.

$$\left(\begin{array}{c} table \\ \rule{3cm}{0.4pt} \\ of\ contents \end{array} \right)$$

Foreword by Dave Bricker i

Introduction 1

1 The Baker's Cake 3

2 My Journey Through Story 13

3 Why This Book? 21

4 The Six Secrets of Connection 27

5 Why Story Works 33

6 Three Points of Connection 41

7 The Story Formula™ Overview and Legend 49

8 Create Your Product Profile 55

9 Create Your Buyer Profile 61

10 Create Your Seller Profile 67

11 Putting it All Together: Craft Your Connection Story 75

12 Happily Ever After 87

Appendix I: Storytelling Tips 89

Appendix II: What We All Want 99

(*introduction*)

You have a story to tell. You may not yet understand its power or its magic. You may not know how to craft it, or tell it, or apply it, but you are here. And I am so glad you are. Our paths were destined to cross. I hope I leave you a little better off than I found you.

While I have been talking about the power of story for decades, the rest of the business world is finally catching on to the fact that storytelling is the magic sauce that helps you connect and engage in business. Understanding how to write and tell stories is one of the most important and coolest skills you can possess in today's business environment.

While a lot of people are talking about how much story matters, not many people actually teach us how to do it! I've even seen speakers talk about storytelling and not tell a single story in the process. Baffling.

I have spent my life and career playing with stories, and I've had the delicious honor of finding that people are willing to listen to me tell them. For years people have come to me for help with their stories. I help make their stories better and give them tips. But something's been missing—something that will help them create stories on their own without my assistance.

It wasn't until a group of scientists gave me the task of helping them write the stories of their products that I was forced to create a formula. After all, what would scientists respect more than a formula?

And here we are. Fifteen years after I started as a wandering storyteller, I have a formula—quite a few in fact. Story is never an exact science, but this comes pretty darned close. And if I can take the art of story and wrap it in a formula, then you have no excuse not to create wonderful stories of your own.

1
THE BAKER'S CAKE

Charlie O'Leary was the resident baker in Prides Hollow for as far back as anybody could remember. His award-winning, butter-filled, sugar-christened creations had stood watch over just about every occasion in town. As people wished him well on his journey into retirement, a few extra tears were shed over the passing of their favorite pastries. For folks in Prides Hollow, food ranked right up there with Jesus and football. Not necessarily in that order.

Enter the new bakery owner—a wide-eyed, overly-eager, thin man from all the way over in *South Carolina*. Who ever heard of a thin baker? That alone was enough to cast suspicion. They had never seen *his* pies at the state fair. Mr. Bean was his name. Put it right there up on the sign! The nerve. Changed the name of the bakery before Charlie O'Leary had even finished getting his stuff out. *Bean's Baked Goods* he called it. Baked goods? Well wasn't that big city fancy? It was quite the topic of gossip for days. Thank goodness, because the tale of Erma the church secretary getting a face lift was wearing pretty thin, and people were realizing she actually seemed a little bit nicer now that her face didn't have an expression. But that's beside the point.

What people didn't know about Mr. Bean was that he was a fresh widow. His wife had died from diabetes. In addition to missing his best friend in the world, Mr. Bean felt an added pressure because he considered himself part of the reason she'd died. He'd been doing some research, and as it turns out, sugar played a big part in taking away the person he loved most in the world. Sugar—the prime ingredient on which Mr. Bean's livelihood was based. You can imagine.

A new dream was born in Mr. Bean—a dream to create a line of sugar-free baked goods, starting with a revolutionary cake. He was so excited. He planned it out—researched the ingredients—and then researched them again. He hired people to help him create the perfect formula—not just sugar free, but organic. And why not add things to make it more vitamin rich? And let's fix joints while we're at it. Mr. Bean was truly creating something that would change the world.

He named his first cake *Healthy Cake*, which didn't win him any awards for creativity, but that's what it was—a healthy cake. Just made sense. His wife would have been proud. It was too late for her, but Mr. Bean knew he could help others. Suddenly his work took on a lot more meaning.

He had been working on this cake for a year when he bought Charlie O'Leary's bakery and moved to Prides Hollow. One week after hanging his new sign, he was ready to unveil his amazing new Healthy Cake. He put it right up front in the display window. He even had a sign made to tell everybody all the things that were—and weren't—in this healthy cake. It was quite a large sign, as most of the ingredients had more than three syllables. He doubled up on supplies to handle the expected explosion in sales.

But the bell on his door only rang a couple of times that day and nobody looked twice at the display. He figured it had to do with the rain, but over the next week, traffic was light, and very few people gave the cake any attention. Some peered closer to take a look at the sign. Others scratched their heads in confusion at the idea that a cake would be brown and chunky. Others just smiled politely and declined when Mr. Bean offered them a sample.

When people turn down a free sample, you have a big problem.

This is ridiculous, Mr. Bean thought. *Do these people not care about being healthy? Half of them have weight problems. The rest have high blood pressure, high cholesterol, bad knees, aching joints. And the ones out there walking and exercising are not paying any attention to what they're eating. I saw one lady buy twice the amount of vitamins she should be taking. It's crazy! I have the answer right here! I can help them! Don't they know sugar is the enemy, not fat? Why won't they listen? I just need to educate them. I'll make sure they know what's in this cake.*

Mr. Bean dedicated himself to making sure every person in town knew the ingredients in his new cake and all that it could do. He had postcards made and passed them around town. He hung them up in the coffee shop—which was experiencing a higher than normal amount of traffic as people had started going there for second-rate pastries. He did everything he knew to do, but the more Mr. Bean tried and the louder he yelled, the more people ignored him. Instead of educating them, he was making them angry. They actually went out of their way to avoid Mr. Bean and his baked goods. He had failed, and he had no idea why.

Charlie O'Leary found Mr. Bean sitting in his bakery on the morning he gave up. I'm thinking Charlie had heard the rumors and took it upon himself to go give a little encouragement to the poor man and his Healthy Cake.

"I don't understand," said Mr. Bean. "Why doesn't anybody want my healthy cake?"

"The problem isn't the cake," said Charlie O'Leary. "There's no question about it—you've created something amazing if it does what you say it'll do. You should be proud. Problem isn't the cake. Problem is how you're selling it. You're too focused on the ingredients. It's not ingredients that sell the cake. It's *you* that sells the cake. People buy from *people,* Mr. Bean. First thing to sell is you. Why should they trust you? Why should they believe you? Why does this matter so much to you? They need to feel that. You've got to make this personal. Then you've got to tell them why it matters so much to *them.* Not in your words, but in theirs. Sell *the story,* Mr. Bean, and your cake will sell by itself.

And it couldn't hurt to make it look a little prettier. Nobody wants a cake that looks like road kill. It's kind of blasphemous if you think about it." And Charlie shuffled off, munching on his free sample of Mr. Bean's Healthy Cake that wasn't actually half bad.

The next day word got out that Mr. Bean was holding an open house and giving out free cupcakes. Cupcakes were friendly, familiar, and old-fashioned enough to rank as a high priority on just about everybody's list—especially given the buttery, sugary pastry famine that had so recently descended upon Prides Hollow as a consequence of Charlie O'Leary's retirement.

When the townsfolk gathered in the bakery to share cupcakes and coffee, Charlie O'Leary stood, cleared his throat and began to speak. "Folks, you've known me a long time. I watched most of you grow up in this town, and we've shared quite a few good memories in this spot. When it came time for me to retire, I was a little worried about who would take my place, until I met Mr. Bean. Mr. Bean here is more than just a good baker; he's a friend. And he has a story behind the work he does. Mr. Bean, would you share with us a little bit about why you created this Healthy Cake of yours. Seems it hasn't really gotten the attention it deserves. We've all heard what's in it. Now why don't you tell us why it matters so much to you and why you should think it could matter to them?

The people in town listened quietly as Mr. Bean shared his heart. He told them about his wife—a woman they would never get to meet—his best friend—the inspiration behind his dreams. He showed them pictures of his children and grandchildren at the beach. He told them about how a while back his wife started having health issues—this pain and that pain—and how it got harder to do things together and how she was having a hard time keeping up with her grandchildren—how she just kept feeling worse and he wasn't able to help. He talked about how they thought they'd be together forever. But forever came sooner than they'd thought.

While folks listened, they could relate to pieces of his story, reminded of times when they'd found themselves in similar situations. They smiled at memories of their own grandchildren at the beach. While their's wasn't the same as Mr. Bean's, some of them thought about their own pain. After just a few moments of Mr. Bean sharing his story, people began to see him in a different way. He wasn't so much a stranger any more. He was one of them.

"We realized what the problem was," Mr. Bean continued. "It was the sugar. For years we had been thinking it was something else. We never knew that we could have done something about her sickness. The answer was right in front of us all along. We saw too late how what we were eating had been hurting us. We listened to the wrong people—not paying attention to the ones who were warning us. Everything she went through could have been avoided if we had only known." The people listening started to feel a little uncomfortable, wondering whether they should be paying more attention—wondering if maybe Mr. Bean knew something they didn't.

"So I decided that even though it's too late to help my wife, it's not too late to help others. I sure do love making pies and cakes, but I loved my wife more. And I think maybe you all care more about being healthy than you realize. And that's what my healthy cake is all about. It might not be the most appealing thing under the glass counter; I'm working on that. But it just might be the one that saves your life. And isn't that worth just a moment of your attention?

"And one more thing…" Mr. Bean smiled at the crowd of new friends standing in his shop. "Are you enjoying the cupcakes?"

Everyone nodded and smiled, and a smattering of applause affirmed their approval. Well, except for Erma, but they blamed her stiff expression on the Botox.

"If you like the cupcakes, they're made from the same ingredients as my Healthy Cakes."

Ernie Smith was so impressed, he placed an order for ten of them right there on the spot. Mr. Bean made a mental note to make up some flyers about moderation.

That night something simple happened. By sharing his story, Mr. Bean changed from being a stranger into someone they felt they could trust—and it wasn't a list of ingredients that did it; it was the story. Mr. Bean hadn't just told his own story, he had told *theirs*. And that, just as Charlie O'Leary had predicted, made all the difference.

That year Mr. Bean's Healthy Cake won first place at the state fair, which came as no surprise, what with all the people who showed up to share a story about how that cake had changed their life.

Charlie O'Leary swears his knees don't hurt anymore since eating that cake. Ruth says she noticed a difference in her child's autism. Old Man Wiley says his cholesterol went down and he doesn't need to take medication anymore. Those are just a few of the stories that sell Mr. Bean's Healthy Cake.

Not a person in town could tell you what's in it.

Mrs. Bean would be proud.

DISCUSSION

1. Why do you think Mr. Bean had such a hard time selling his cake?
   How did the people in town feel about Mr. Bean?
   Did that affect his ability to sell his cake?

2. What do you think made people start buying his cake?
   What do you think Charlie O'Leary meant when he said "sell the story?"

3. Why do you think I chose to tell you this story? What purpose does this story serve for me as your teacher? Couldn't I just have told you that stories are important? Would that have been as effective?

4. How does this story apply to you? What can you take away and use from it to help in your own business?

5. What is the "Healthy Cake" that you have to share with the world?

6. Are you selling the ingredients or the story of your healthy cake?
   What do people think about you? Are you a Charlie O'Leary or a Mr. Bean?

7. How well do you know the people who should buy your healthy cake?

NOTES

NOTES

2
MY JOURNEY THROUGH STORY

Pink Zebra

I was tucking my young son into bed. We'd been through the usual drill—bedtime story, glass of water, bathroom trip, monster check, and a rambling prayer that would have made Moses proud. I was ready to flip the switch on another day of Mommy-hood and relax for a while. My best friend, Chardonnay, was waiting for me in the kitchen. She's a good friend. She was friends with my mother first. She's the reason I had kids.

I was about to turn off the light when my son called out, "Mom? Why do zebras have stripes?" He picks his most challenging questions to ask at bedtime. It's his gift. But this time I had the answer, or at least thought I did.

"Zebras have stripes so they'll blend into the pack," I told him. "You don't want to be a pink zebra, or a predator will find you and eat you alive!" (Note to self: not a good bedtime story.) I spoke from experience, because I had spent my whole life being the pink zebra, the one who didn't fit, the one who zigged when everybody zagged, the one who couldn't seem to color in the lines or play by the rules.

I grew up believing that to be happy, successful, and content, you had to be like everybody else—blend in or die—so I took everything I had that made me wonderfully unique, and threw it away. I spent most of my years painting over my pink.

Turns out I'm not the only one.

Were you pink too?

Are you still trying to cover it up?

Don't.

We like pink.

This Weird Gift

Because I didn't have friends of my own, I created them. The characters I wrote about in my stories kept me company. They made me laugh, encouraged me, taught me, and became my greatest source of strength. It's amazing what we reveal when we put our hearts on paper. My heart was stolen by a town called Prides Hollow and a wacky cast of characters who have been with me every step of my journey—even while hiding under my fear that they wouldn't be good enough. They were still there whispering.

I have spent much of my life lost in books. The more I read, the better I write. To this day, it is such a thrill to step into someone else's story. Standing in it, experiencing the romance, the thrill, the suspense—connecting with the character who mirrors our pain and desires in life. I have read books that have changed my life, and heard stories that forever impacted the way I see myself and the world around me.

Your stories will do that for people. No matter how simple or ordinary they may seem, your stories have that same power. Later we'll talk more about that—a lot.

But back to me.

Storytelling was my gift from an early age. It never occurred to me, or anyone else, really, that it would become anything more than just a little hobby. Who knew that the thing that made me weird would become the thing that would become my calling? The people in Prides Hollow did. They always believed even when I didn't.

And Then Fate Stepped In

Storytelling remained my private obsession until after college when I took a writing class at a local community college with a group of teachers seeking continued education credits. Our assignment was to read an original story to the class. My classmates told me my story was good, but the way I told it was magical.

They invited me to their schools to tell stories to the kids. I had one story prepared for children, written on about thirty-eight index cards lined up on the floor. I didn't realize I wouldn't be able to see them, but it didn't matter. I was hooked. That twenty-five-dollar check was the most beautiful thing I had ever seen.

I soon realized that children were not my ideal market. I was also speaking to the teachers—to the adults in the room. They stopped working on their lesson plans and followed me into my town. It was at one of these schools that I met an art teacher who was a professional storyteller. Who knew there was such a thing? She led me to an entire community of professional storytellers. The folks in Prides Hollow were beside themselves with joy. They had finally found a place where they could walk in the open.

"You Have a Gift!"

When I met my husband Bill and dragged him into Prides Hollow, he became my biggest fan. He was the first one to say out loud, "You have a gift. You can do something others can't. You can get paid for this." Thanks, Bill. Who knew where that road would take us, eh? We had no idea what lay ahead.

We began to treat my gift as more than a hobby. We began to treat it like a business.

I wrote this book to help you treat storytelling like a business. To help you have more impact and influence in your world. To help you tell your story in a way that connects to your listener.

Easier Said Than Done

It's one thing to call yourself a professional storyteller. It's another to actually make money doing it. Talk about a hard sell. There's not a big market out there for clients wanting to pay you to come tell stories, no matter how good you think you are.

That's when fate stepped in again to steer me straight.

But first, a side note: That's the thing about dreams. They don't always work out the way you envision. They don't always sell. Sometimes you have to let a dream take a new shape. That's what I had to do. Maybe you will, too. Just keep at it. Fate has a way of stepping in when you need it. Shoot. Maybe that's why you bought this book?

Fate is a Tall Lady With Silver Hair

I was telling stories at a festival in North Carolina, when a tall, silver-haired, beautiful woman came up to my product table to ask me questions about the world of storytelling. We were both here to work at the festival. I was the hired storyteller; she was the hired speaker. We both did the same thing, just under a different label; we both told funny stories. Her name was Jeanne Robertson, and meeting her changed the course of my business and the course of my life. She showed me where I belonged. That was the day I became a motivational speaker. The people in Prides Hollow were excited and then a little afraid. With good reason. They were about to be buried alive.

Fear Strikes Again

Twelve years ago I took my stories and jumped into the world of professional speaking. I took one look around and decided I didn't belong—not like this. In my typical fashion, I began to paint over my pink. I took my town and my characters and buried them under the excuse that they didn't belong in this world. Shame on me. I took the very thing I had that would have made me instantly, refreshingly unique, and covered it up. I became like the other black and white zebras, and set out to blend. The folks in Prides Hollow were so angry they didn't speak to me for almost a year.

I became a successful speaker. I told stories. But the vision of what I wanted to create had been cast aside—until now. It's back. They're back. Bigger and bolder than ever.

Because if there's one thing I've learned, it's that blending in doesn't get you noticed.

Blending in doesn't help you stand out among the competition.

Blending in is the kiss of death.

Nobody notices normal.

Being pink is a good thing.

Being pink is everything.

Trust me.

Embrace your pink.

The Power of Connection

In the beginning my stories were just for entertaining people. I would make them laugh, encourage them, take them on a journey. Every kind of story had the power to hold their attention. They weren't texting. They weren't getting up to go to the bathroom. They weren't checking their watches. They weren't sleeping. (Okay, so in the nursing home they were sleeping, but still.) I began to see the charm of taking the written word and performing it—of bringing the story to life, bringing the audience into the story. Because that's what storytelling is—it's a shared conversation—a connection between you and the audience through the stories you share.

I began to see that my ability to tell a story was accomplishing something far more impactful than just entertaining people. I was sending audiences away with something—something that changed their lives, something gave them a new perspective, something that whispered encouragement and hope into their ears, belief, inspiration. Every story I told had the delicious opportunity to speak truth.

I studied the art of connection. How could I structure my words in a way that made people think, act, and feel motivated? I watched influencers of all kinds—from speakers to preachers to politicians to musicians to salespeople and business leaders—anyone with a platform and a voice. I looked for patterns that would help me master the art of connection and engagement with my audience.

Once I understood how to go from entertainment to connection, my business soared. I was onto something.

DISCUSSION

1. Can you relate to being a pink zebra?

2. Did you think about your own life as you read this story?

3. Do you feel like you know me better now? Be honest. Are you more or less interested in what I have to say?

4. I could have just given you a book of rules and advice, but I started with my own story. Does that help? How?

5. How important is it for you to feel like you know something about the author when you're reading non-fiction?

NOTES

3
WHY THIS BOOK?

I once met with two men from another country to discuss the idea of collaborating on a project that involved a merging of our brands. I was a little nervous because I didn't know them very well. I was worried the meeting might be a scam. Or perhaps they wanted to marry me? Don't laugh—I've received quite a few offers on Facebook.

The beginning of our video chat was a little awkward. We sat there looking at each other, waiting to see who would speak first. Me and my big fat southern accent, and two men from Eastern Europe made an awkward combination (You write the jokes). The last person to enter the call was the owner and founder of the company I was meeting with. He jumped into the conversation by apologizing for being late, and for showing up in a jogging suit. He explained that normally he would be in business attire, but it was his day to pick his children up from school and take them to the park. "Today is my son's birthday," he explained, pointing to the birthday banner behind him. In that moment, I became more comfortable. He was a dad. He had kids. He took them to the park. That was enough for me to see that he wasn't so different from me. And we were off.

What happened in those opening moments is critical to the relationship between Seller and Buyer. A connection was made—human to human. He became likeable and trustworthy. We found common ground. That's what this book is about—finding common ground between ourselves, our messages, and the people we want to influence—and using story to do it.

We're All Salespeople

I never considered myself a salesperson in the usual business sense. When I think of a salesperson, I think of a guy spending all week on planes, wearing an ordinary suit and sensible shoes, giving a presentation in front of a flip chart, and then heading to the bar to drink liquor straight and pick up women. Okay, so I watch too many movies. Salespeople *sell*. I'm an artist; I tell stories. But selling is as much a part of my job as any other job. When I stand on stages and tell stories, I'm selling—I'm selling *me*. I sell the people in my audience on the idea that they can see beyond their obstacles. I sell my information. And here you are reading this book—just sayin'.

When I became a mom, I entered into the most challenging sales job of all. I have a college degree. I consider myself fairly smart. But nothing was as hard as trying to convince my son to use the potty. He won every time. To this day, he is the ultimate negotiator, and I won't admit which of us wins more negotiations (though you'll be glad to know I did finally win the potty war).

We all want to influence someone else, whether it's to get a job, win a promotion, sell a product, manage people, serve customers, give speeches, lead teams, coach little league, raise awareness, lead change, empower women, inspire a congregation, convince your spouse that you need a new car, or get your kid to clean up his room. All of us, at one time or another, want to influence someone else. That makes us salespeople.

You probably know the cardinal rule of sales: People buy from people they like, trust, believe, and feel like they know. Take a look at those words for a moment:

LIKE
TRUST
BELIEVE
KNOW

Every one of these words has to do with how you *feel* about someone else. These words are about *emotions*.

"I can't explain it; I just like the guy."

"Normally, no, but I have good feeling about you. Just pay me back by Friday."

"I don't know why, but I don't believe a word that candidate is saying."

"When I drop the baby off with Mary, I know she's in good hands."

Too many people who seek to impact others, skip over these four words. They head right into telling me what I should do, without getting to know me first.

People don't want to be told what to do. If you want to convince / persuade / inspire / motivate / encourage / impact / lead, you'd better get them to like you, trust you, believe you, and feel like they know you.

Data Can't Evoke Emotion

To impact results and influence people, you must be able to create an emotional connection with your listener. What you know—how smart you are, your facts and figures, your information, your credentials, and your slick promotional materials—can't create emotional impact. Too many people rely on data to sell, and wonder why nobody is paying attention. Too many people push themselves on their market, instead of pulling their market to them. Too many people kill us with data. Selling is all about relationships. Impacting and influencing your world is not about communication; it's about *connection*.

Facts Push • Emotion Pulls

In a crowded market it's not about being heard above the noise, but being trusted.

Why This Book?

This book will help you master the art of connection and engagement through the power of strategic storytelling. You're probably thinking, "Just give me the formula already!" but the formula won't work unless you understand the logic behind it. If becoming a wizard was as simple as buying a wand, you would already have one. This book is where you learn about *magic*. The key to crafting stories that have impact is to understand how stories work.

Moving forward, I'm going to refer to you as the Seller, to the person you are trying to influence as the Buyer, and to what you are selling as the Product—even if you aren't really selling a tangible product, but a truth or a lesson or a concept.

Seller = You

Buyer = Who You Want to Influence

Product = Your Product or Message

DISCUSSION

1. Who are you trying to impact, and how much do they like you? Trust you? Believe you? Feel like they know you?

2. Think of the people you do business with in your personal life. Would you do business with a jerk? Would you buy from someone who lies?

3. When you're looking for a product or need to hire a professional, why do you ask your friends for advice?

4. Why do you think so much business is based on referral and word-of-mouth?

5. What are you doing to connect and engage with customers and colleagues?

6. People buy based on emotion. How do you make people feel?

NOTES

4

THE SIX SECRETS OF CONNECTION

What's the goal?
To connect and engage.

Is connection about facts and figures?
Connection is all about emotion.

Does your data make you likeable, trustworthy, believable, or different?
What does?

During the years I have studied the art of connection, I have identified six principles that create a connection between buyer and seller.

I remember in the early days of my storytelling career when I got to open up for Loretta Lynn. It was so exciting. My husband and I stayed up most of the night printing labels for the cassette tapes I was sure would sell out. Before the show started, we stood in the lobby with the rest of the people who couldn't get in. I stood there proudly behind my product table while a team of people in black rushed around Loretta Lynn's table selling merchandise. Compared to her, I looked like a lemonade stand.

A tall, burly gentleman approached my table wearing a biker's jacket and a smirk. His arms were crossed as he looked down his nose at my cassette tapes and sneered, "Kelly Swanson? I've never heard of her!" And with a snort he walked off. It wasn't my proudest moment.

After the show (it went well; thanks for asking) I rushed back to the lobby to wait for the mob of people to come pouring out of the theater. They ran right to Loretta's booth. I stood there thinking it might actually have been more lucrative to sell lemonade, when the burly biker jacket guy came back up to my table. This time he came around to the back of the table and got right in my comfort zone. But this time his arms were not crossed. "Two hours ago, I didn't know who you were" he said, 'but now I will remember you forever." He wrapped me up in a giant hug. While my face was smooshed up under his arm like a puppy, it occurred to me that something had happened between me and him—something I've watched happen over and over for years—the power of connecting with another human being.

I will always be amazed that I can come in front of a group of strangers, spend only an hour with them, and change their lives forever—people I have nothing in common with—people from different parts of the world—people who start off thinking they can't relate to me at all. If I can do it, so can you.

Here are my secrets:

1. Humor

Laughter is the Quickest Way into a Stranger's Heart

Aspiring speakers often ask me if they need to be funny to succeed. The answer is no, but your audience does need to laugh. Laughs are currency. We are paid as speakers to deliver an experience, and laughter is one way to make it unforgettable. You don't have to be a standup comic, and I don't recommend doing something that is unnatural for you. Instead of focusing on being funny, focus on being *fun*.

How's your funny bone? Can you add a little more fun to your message?

I won't go deep into humor in this book. I already have a workbook that serves that purpose. It's called "Humor CPR" and you can find it on Amazon.

2. Humility
They Don't Connect to Perfection, but rather to Imperfection

The speaking business is filled with people who brag about going from earning zero to six figures of income in less than a year. There is no shortage of Facebook selfies posed in front of fancy houses and sports cars with taglines that say "This could be you!" I have never seen more people openly claim to be the "world's most sought after" in a world that has no idea who they are—claiming to be experts in an industry that has no idea they exist. I am amazed at how many speakers openly boast on social media about how good they are, forgetting that a true professional would *never* walk up to a group and start telling them how much money they make and how big their last audience was. That is no way to make friends and form deeper connections. Yuck.

Someone once advised me that as a speaker I should never act like I don't have all the answers. Someone else advised me to "look the part"—meaning I had to invest in a thousand-dollar suit. Not my style. My style is not to come before your group and make sure you realize how high above you I am. My goal is to make sure you realize *I'm one of you.* I don't scream my own praises or claim perfection. In fact, I claim imperfection—almost as a personal brand—and this is what makes me connect with audiences wherever I go. It is my secret weapon. The worse I get, the more they love me. It is quite possible to find a happy balance between humility and honoring your achievements.

How are you at admitting a little vulnerability once in a while? Try it. You might be surprised. Flaws don't make you weak; they make you human and relatable.

3. Humanity
They Don't Care How Much You Know Until They Know How Much You Care.

'Humanity' is a word I associate with serving others. Connection is personal, and one step deeper than just how they feel about you. True magic happens when you change how people feel about themselves. That's the secret sauce for motivating and influencing. Connection is about serving your listener. You're here for *them,* not for you. If you're thinking about quotas and commissions, your sales prospects will smell your self-absorption from across the room.

Focus on what they need to hear, not on what you want to say.

What does your Buyer need to hear? We'll get into this later.

4. Passion
It's Hard to Define, But You Know it When You See it.

It's hard to teach passion or even define it, but you know when someone has it and when they don't. Passion is about being excited by and interested in what you are talking about. It's about believing that what you have to say can change lives. If you deliver your sales pitch the same way you do your grocery list, you will fail. If you disconnect from the passion, so will your customers. Sometimes people feel passionate about a message, but they don't know how to turn that into words, or deliver it in a way that reveals that passion. It takes work—no question about it—but passion is contagious.

How passionate are you about your Product? Do you expect Buyers to be excited about something you lost interest in?

5. Authenticity
In A Crowded Market, Nobody Notices Normal

If there is one thing I've learned about connecting, it's that *different* gets attention, especially when you're different with value attached. Riding in on a unicycle is just a cheap trick unless the unicycle ties into your message. No offense unicycle speakers.

The easiest path to different is authenticity. So many speakers think the key is in copying other speakers, when the truth is that the magic sauce already exists in who you are as an individual. Bring that authentic person to the stage and you will stand out in the crowd. I promise. Luckily, the crowded market is filled with chorus line competitors—all doing the same thing—kicking their legs at the same angle. It's easy to do one tiny thing that sets you apart. Your audience will thank you.

What's your Authenticity Factor? Got a little weird in you?

6. Story

Facts Compel, but Stories SELL

Ah, this one is my favorite. This is where I spend all of my time. This is where we'll stay for the rest of the book. The reason I went from zero to six figures in a year—okay, ten years—was because I know how to tell a good story. Story is the tool that allows you to accomplish humor, humility, humanity, passion, authenticity and more. Data and points and information don't have the ability to connect. Facts have no emotion, but connection is all about emotion. Data isn't emotional. People are. Therefore, stories have the ability to connect on an emotional level because you connect to the people in a story and their pain. We can't connect to the story of a company that was started in 1920. We connect to a man who had a dream in 1920 of building something great.

You've watched speakers focus on giving the audience as many facts as possible. Not only were you falling asleep after ten minutes, you were disengaged, and not the least bit motivated to act on this new information or even believe it. Information is only as good as the way it's wrapped and delivered to us—the experience. If you just give me facts, you are a lecturer—and not a very good one.

The best teachers we had in school were the ones who brought knowledge to life. They wrapped it in an experience. They wrapped it in story.

Are you killing your Buyer with data? Don't worry. By the end of this book, you'll be well on your way to mastering the magic power of storytelling.

NOTES

5
WHY STORY WORKS

I spoke to a group of HR people on the value of story to engage employees. I began my presentation by stating the current Gallup Poll statistic on disengaged employees in the workforce. Then I told them this story:.

You could hear her singing all the way from the parking lot. *Some sweet morning, when this day is over, I'll fly away*—loud, staccato, jubilant notes of a life well lived. The glass automatic doors opened and I could see her standing there, holding her mop as if it were a beloved dance partner, as if her faded cotton dress were made of the finest silk. I sat in the corner of the lobby, trying not to stare at this woman who was oblivious to everyone around her, as if it were the most normal thing in the world to be singing and twirling her way across the marbled floors of a hospital lobby while the beeps of the monitors and the dings of the elevators sang to her in sweet harmony. I could smell the perfume of my changed perspective as I watched this woman turn her job into an art—turn her work into an act of worship.

She didn't know I was in the restroom, close enough to hear her stop working to go pray for a stranger's wounded child. She didn't see me standing there watching her help that old man wrap the blanket tighter around his wife's shoulders. She didn't know I saw her give away her lunch. So many moments throughout that day, I watched as her songs, her smile, her very aura, affected everyone who crossed her path. I watched as in those cold, unexpecting, antiseptic corners of that hospital, pain found healing, sorrow found comfort, hopelessness found hope—wrapped in a faded cotton dress and comfortable shoes.

You could hear her singing all the way to the parking lot when she went to meet her bus at dusk. I stood by the large glass window and watched her go, wishing she wouldn't, wondering if I would ever see her again, knowing I would never forget her.

Just outside that window hung a large, slick, commercialized sign that had no doubt been created by a group of marketing intellectuals: "Excellence starts here." I wondered if the CEO knew just how true that really was. That day a woman with a mop had changed my perspective. A woman who smelled of bleach and blessings showed me how I want to serve my customers. And, the funny thing was she had no idea.

If a woman with a mop can find a way to sing—why can't we?

At the end of the presentation (two hours later) I asked my audience how many people could remember the statistic I gave them at the beginning of my talk. A couple of hands went up, and I think they both remembered wrong. Then I asked how many people could remember the song the woman with the mop was singing? Almost every hand went up. That's the power of story. The stories you use to engage with will be the pieces they remember the most, and will have the biggest impact.

Here are some things that story alone was able to accomplish in my presentation:

- **Entertain my audience.** People love a good story. Period. Sometimes their mind wanders when I'm deep in content. But when I'm in story, nobody moves.

- **Engage my audience.** Engagement is about involving your audience. When you tell a story they step into your space. That's interaction, even when they don't say a word.

- **Show instead of tell.** I can tell people in the audience how to deliver good customer service, or I can tell them this story. Telling people what to do has a pushing action. Story has a pulling action.

- **Relate to my audience.** I don't have any idea what it's like to work in maintenance, but when I told that story to people who do, they felt like I "got" them. We had a common connection. One man told me that he was "the woman with the mop," and nobody had ever taken the time to tell him he was appreciated. Sniff. Sniff. (And technically I didn't tell him that; the woman with the mop did.)

- **Create trust with my audience.** The value of the story is transferred to the teller. If I tell you the story of my grandfather and how honest he was, you're going to assume that I value honesty. This *shows* you something about me, instead of just *telling* you.

- **Show appreciation in a lasting way.** When someone in your audience can find common ground with the main character in your story, and that character is honored, then your listener feels honored and understood.

- **Teach a truth or explain a concept.** I was helping a businessperson create his pitch to let people know what he does. His service is high-tech computer oriented, and his clients usually know nothing about computers. He speaks an entirely different language from his listener. We had to find a common ground story that could connect his business concept with something his listeners could understand.

We crafted a simple story about a commercial refrigerator in a restaurant and the employees who kept buying items for the refrigerator without taking inventory of what was already in there. Items would get shoved to the back of the fridge, people would buy more of something they already had, and it cost the restaurant a lot of money they didn't even realize they were losing.

That is what is happening in our computers. Somebody needs to come clean out the fridge. That was this guy's job. The story was crafted better than that, but you get the point. We found a story everybody in the room could relate to to explain a concept they were unfamiliar with. They don't need to understand how the computer works. They just get it. It's like the refrigerator.

By the way, even though I still don't understand what this guy does, I believe he can do it because I can visualize the story of the fridge. Isn't that interesting? For all we know the analogy is nothing like what he does.

These are just a few of the things story can do. Can you see why I'm such a big fan? By the end of this book, you will be too.

THE SCIENCE BEHIND STORY

Science has proven that we don't take any action without having a visual "image" of that action (In this case, an "image" can also mean the memory of a sound, smell, taste, or feeling). We don't act without "seeing" it in our head. Thoughts are not stored as words; they are stored as images. Therefore, if we want our facts to have a lasting impact on our listener, we need to wrap them in images. Having information delivered as an image gives your listener a way to step inside the truth, test drive your message, experience your lesson, and come to their own conclusions instead of being force-fed. Leave an image behind to reside in your Buyer's mental library to access and act on later.

From the beginning of our lives we are taught through stories. Faith is shared through stories. History starts with cavemen sharing stories through images scrawled on cave walls. We use story pictures to illustrate points. Teachers have students conduct experiments to experience facts as they apply to life—to create images to connect with the facts they learn.

My son is home-schooled, and stories are the most powerful tool we have to help him understand concepts. He understands the facts of history because he has read the stories of the people who lived it. We even explain math to him in the form of a story. He has a hard time learning vocabulary words and definitions until I give him the context (story) of the word as it applies to life. Until I give him a story, they are just random words that don't make sense because he has never seen an image of them in action. The story helps us learn and remember what the word means.

The concept of using story to teach is nothing new. We just don't often think of its importance in business as a tool of impact and influence. We think we don't have time to tell stories—that our clients only care about the facts. Facts are important—very important—but story is the context within which we deliver our facts memorably.

The first key to being able to use story to your advantage, is to understand why it works—that it is a tool. You need to know what the tool is for, before you can use it effectively.

An old Yiddish parable has been passed around for years and quoted by many in different versions. It explains the power of story:

TRUTH, naked and cold, had been turned away from every door in the village. Her nakedness frightened the people. When PARABLE found her she was huddled in a corner, shivering and hungry. Taking pity on her, PARABLE gathered her up and took her home. There, she dressed TRUTH in story, warmed her, and sent her out again. Clothed in story, TRUTH knocked again at the doors and was readily welcomed into the villagers' houses. They invited her to eat at their tables and warm herself by their fires.

Your Product Information (Truth) is uninteresting and unappealing (Naked and Cold) until you wrap it in Story (Parable). Once it's wrapped in story, your Buyer won't just accept it; they will invite it in.

CLOTHING TRUTH IN STORY IS THE WAY TO CONNECT WITH YOUR BUYER.

FACTS PUSH. STORIES PULL.

DISCUSSION

1. Can you think of a story you used to teach your child, or one your parent used to teach you? How did story impact behavior? How long have you remembered that story?

2. What is your Product? Your Truth? Your Lesson? Your Message? Your Service? The Concept? The Brand? The Cause? The Gift you have to share with the world? Can you identify what that is?

3. Is your Truth naked and cold, or have you wrapped it in Parable?

4. Where are the places and platforms that you have to share your Truth, anywhere you have a touch point with your listener? There may be more than you realize. As salespeople we often think that the place to share our truth is in the sales presentation, but our platform is so much bigger than that.

NOTES

6
THREE POINTS OF CONNECTION

I speak at a lot of women's health events (I'll pause while you gasp in shock). Yes, it appears I have become the poster child for women's health. Apparently I'm the cautionary tale. Over the years, I have watched thousands of health presentations and been on the receiving end of many pitches for supplements by the scientists who created them. I learned a lot from these scientists about the art of connection, or lack of it. These scientists were highly respected men and women in their fields. They had worked to find cures and preventions for various health issues. I'm sure they all believed in the products they were telling me about. Some had spent ten years developing and researching their ideas; I imagine they were pretty invested—or at least I assumed they were. But it was hard to tell by their expressions and the absolute lack of excitement in their presentations as they stood in the dark under data-filled screens and *read to us*—word for word for word for word.

I got a lot of rest at those conferences, and I'm pretty sure the audience did too. I watched people around me checking Facebook, sending emails, chatting with neighbors, writing out grocery lists, digging through purses for food, and even snoring.

I sat at one conference on a Saturday, listening to scientists pitch products to a room full of buyers and potential sellers. I was scheduled to speak at the end of the day, but decided to come at 8am and listen to the other speakers. By 9am I regretted that decision. In just one hour, I felt like I had landed on another planet filled with people speaking a different language. Seriously. I didn't understand a word. There were *a lot* of words—big words—screens full of them. Every presenter's voice droned on in the same monotone. If the military ever runs out of torture techniques, I have a pretty good suggestion. We were about five presenters in (I'm guessing; I'd lost count) when I woke up and leaned in.

She was an average looking woman dressed in a lab coat like the others, but she was different. She told a joke. She told us about working as an army nurse. In minutes, she became human to me. She had my attention. She, too, had created a solution, but she didn't start with that. She started with the problem—a problem that many people are experiencing, and the effects it has on their lives. She talked about what this problem meant to her in her life, and why it was so important to her to find a solution. (Remember Mr. Bean and his Healthy Cake?) She showed a slide listing all the symptoms of a gut disease she had spent her life studying.

In that moment I slipped from her story into mine. *I had every symptom on her screen.* She was telling *my* story. She had my undivided attention. When her presentation was over, I ran to find her in the hallway and begged her to sell me her product. Within twenty-four hours, I spent three hundred dollars on a solution to my problem. To this day, I can't tell you one thing that's in it. I can't explain to other people how it works. Reading the brochure that explains the product takes me all day; it could be in French considering how little I understand it. Yet this woman impacted and influenced me, in the middle of a crowded market, to pay attention. Why?

- **She made this personal. She went from random scientist to someone I felt I could trust.**
- **She didn't sell me the data; she sold me a *transformation*.**

- **I didn't buy a product; I bought its meaning in my own life.**

It is said that in literature there is really only one theme—the search for meaning. We want to buy things (ideas, visions, products, services, politicians) that mean something to us.

The mistake most people make when trying to influence others is that they focus on the *data*. They focus on what is *necessary*. They focus only on *results*. For true connection you have to take it a step further.

Necessary → Meaningful

Move from necessary to meaningful.

"This water filter removes harmful bacteria and toxins from your drinking water" focuses on something important and *necessary*. "This water filter will help ensure that you and your family stay healthy" is *meaningful*.

Data → Transformation

Move from explaining data to explaining the impact of that data.

"Clinical trial data showed a 75% remission rate in a sample of 1000 Stage IV cancer patients over one year." We should only hope for results like that, but "Three out of four patients were completely cured" is *meaningful* because it speaks directly to the patient's desperately hoped-for *transformation*.

Conflict → Transformation

Move from problems to solutions.

"Our software catches spelling and grammar mistakes, duplicate words, and weak writing style." This statement focuses on *problems*. "This software will make you a better writer. Gain credibility by communicating like a professional." This addresses the *meaningful outcome*.

Your Story ➜ *Their* Story

Move from talking about yourself to talking abut them.

"Our company has been around for 110 years, and we're still winning awards" is all about *you*. "We've been around for over a century, and we will be there to keep your investments safe a hundred years from now" reframes your longevity in terms of its *value to the customer.*

Story is the Bridge

Story does what data can't. Why? Because stories show instead of tell. True impact doesn't happen because you told somebody what to do. It occurs when your listener wants to take action. Stories have the power to convince and persuade on an emotional level. Data can't. Story is the tool that does the work, and then data drives it home.

I've already mentioned this, but it needs to be imprinted in your brain because your tendency will be to walk away and go right back to data again. I've seen it happen hundreds of times. Especially if you're a scientist or product developer, your focus will have been on *mechanics*—on producing results. This may be where you feel naturally strong and comfortable discussing your work. Reframing all of that in the language of storytelling may feel uncomfortable at first, but as you work to see your product in terms of stories, you may discover a surprising new level of meaning and value in it. And despite my "wizard's magic powers" analogy, this is communication science. The Story Formula™ and its various components are logical and sensible.

Wrap Data in Story.

DATA + STORY = CONNECTION

The scientist who won my heart had mastered The Story Formula™. She had successfully completed the three prongs of connection:

(1) Seller Story

(2) Product Story

(3) Customer Story

If you're not getting the sales you could be, if your leadership skills fall short, if your customers don't come back, if your presentations put people to sleep, if you're not being heard in a crowded market, it is because you are not practicing the art of connection. You are missing one or more pieces of The Story Formula™.

As a speaker, I have been hired by hundreds of companies to help motivate their people—to help them deal with stress and change—to help them engage and reconnect to a vision of what they do and why they do it. I get hired to motivate them, but the truth is that people can't be motivated externally—not really. Motivation has to come from within. I can only give people tools to help them change the way they see themselves, their jobs, their co-workers and customers, their situations, and their world. (Wow, that's a lot of stuff; I should charge more.)

Nothing I teach matters until I connect and engage on an emotional level. Even when I'm speaking to a group on how to write a sales pitch, I have to connect and engage on an emotional level to impact and influence. I know I'm saying that again. I'm making sure you don't forget. They say we have to hear something seven times before it sticks, so I probably have a few more times left.

By the time you finish this book, you'll know the Story Formula™, you'll have the blueprint to master it, and you'll have your three critical stories of impact. But more important, you'll have a new skill (storytelling) that will serve you for a lifetime and raise your level of influence.

Sellers who aren't using The Story Formula™. Look something like this:

- The speaker who does nothing but talk about himself and his story is so self-absorbed that he forgets you are even there. I'm pretty sure we've all been on dates like that, right?

- A speaker who jumps right into the data and spends an hour telling you everything you need to do. (Only the Product/Solution Story here.)

- A speaker who just talks in terms of data and solution without relating it to me or them. Like they're a talking head.

A presentation, message, speech, pitch, ad—whatever means you're using to send a message to your listener—must tell all three stories at once. All three languages (Buyer, Seller, Customer) must be spoken to achieve true connection.

I once coached a speaker whose message was about forgiveness. He has a powerful life story about how he learned to forgive someone through a tragic situation in his own life, and how that ability to forgive has helped him create a better life and a better business for himself. He wants to teach people how to forgive.

"I'm afraid that forgiveness won't sell," he told me in our first session. "I'm afraid corporate won't buy it."

"They won't," I answered.

"Should I change my topic?" he asked.

"Heck no! It's cool," I responded. "You're just not telling the third story; it's missing. You're not telling the customer's story. Forgiveness is your solution, but they don't think they need that. Find out what problems they have where forgiveness is the answer. Then you'll have made your connection."

This speaker's Seller Story was great—the story of how he personally learned about forgiveness—why it matters so much to him personally. It's the piece that allows us to connect to and engage with him personally. Like, trust, believe, know—personal. Connection is personal. Personal is emotional.

His Product Story (Message) was great—the art of forgiveness and how we can incorporate that into our lives step by step. He just needed that third piece to complete the connection triangle: The Buyer Story—*what this means* to his audience members and their lives, and how it fits into the pain they experience or the pleasure they seek—the story of what their lives will look like if they change. The Buyer doesn't wake up in the morning saying, "I really need to go learn about forgiveness today." The Buyer wakes up wishing their team didn't fight all the time.

These three points of connection are the foundation for everything I teach. These three "languages" are the reason why pitches succeed or fail, why web copy works or doesn't, why presentations are remembered or forgotten, why products sell or don't, why politicians are voted in or out.

RECAP

GOAL: To connect and engage.
MISSION: To be the interpreter between the product and what it means to the Buyer.
HOW?: Three Connection Stories (Buyer, Seller, Product)
TOOL: Story.

DISCUSSION

Take a moment to think about the three different languages and how they apply to your business.

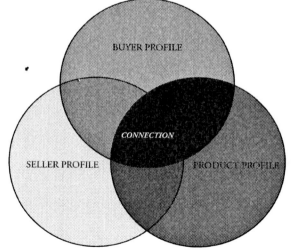

NOTES

Next, we'll dig deep into the formulas that will help you create all three Connection Stories.

7
THE STORY FORMULA™
OVERVIEW AND LEGEND

OVERVIEW

End Goal: Connection Between Buyer, Product, and Seller

1. Create Your Product Profile
2. Create Seller Profile
3. Create Buyer Profile
4. Craft the Connection Story Script
5. Practice the Delivery
6. Plan the Application based on Platform

LEGEND

s   Seller, Trusted Source, Person Doing the Persuading

b   Buyer, Audience, Listener, Person You Want To Persuade

p	Product, Solution, Answer, Content, Message, Truth, What You're Selling
sp	Seller Profile
bp	Buyer Profile
pp	Product Profile
w	What it is/does
y	Why It Matters
cg	Common Ground
c	Connection
ce	Connection and Engagement
cs	Connection Story
i	Intellect, Mind, Thoughts, Speaking to the Mind, Data, Information
e	Emotion, Heart, Feelings, Speaking to Heart, Connection, Engagement

7

LOVE THE STORY = LOVE THE PRODUCT

8

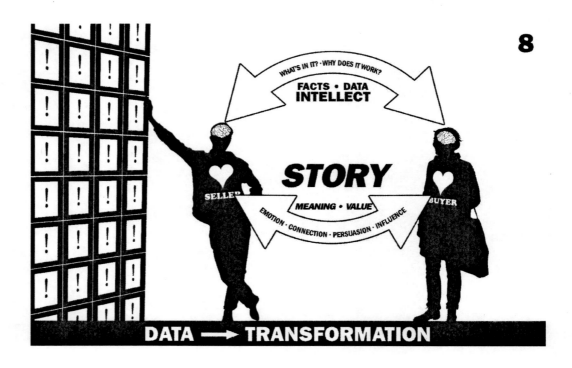

8
CREATE YOUR PRODUCT PROFILE

When I was a child my stories were the creation of my muse. I didn't think about what I was going to write; I just wrote. I didn't plan what was going to happen; I just let the story unfold. That's great for novelists, but when it comes to using strategic storytelling as a tool in business, that method is crap. This isn't a course on writing the next great piece of literature. This is about using words to influence and tap into emotion. And most of us don't have a lot of time or space to do it. We must be able to get in and out quickly with as much impact as possible.

Once writing became my profession and paying my bills depended on it, I no longer had the luxury of waiting on my creative muse to show up, and time to spend hoping she created something worthwhile.

Once I realized people liked funny, I needed to learn how to create more of it.

Once one presentation turned into hundreds, I needed more material.

Once I found out clients liked me to customize my presentation, one stock keynote was not enough.

Once I realized I had to write articles and blogs and social media posts to attract business, I found myself needing to write every day.

Once I had a community built up and a newsletter list formed, I had to feed my guppies.

My creative muse couldn't keep up. I had to let her go. She now has an office in the basement, and only comes around on holidays. I had to figure out how to churn out effective stories on a regular basis. This is where the art truly became a business. I needed stories that *worked* and a method that didn't take all day or depend on a muse.

So do you.

The major flaw in my original writing method was that I let the story control me. *Now, I control the story.* There is a *big* difference. The way you control a story is by planning it out before you write it. Very few people who use story as a tool in business take the extra step of planning the story first; they wing it. Maybe it works for them, but I doubt it. When we plan our stories and craft them according to our plan, we hit magic. It's like a song. You can write a song on the fly that has a bunch of random notes and words strung together, and it may sound pretty when you're done, but when you take the time to craft each note, figure out where it should be placed, and think about the theme and style of the song, the audience will like your music better.

Words have power: Where they are placed. How they are used. Which words you choose. They all make a difference. Taking even one tiny step to craft those words will make a big difference in your finished piece. And, remember, this isn't about a finished piece that just entertains. This is about a finished piece that reaches right into your Buyer's heart and grabs them forever. That's the difference a word can make.

Control the story; don't let the story control you.

Story control is the purpose of the following profile exercises. It's similar to product development techniques scientists use. This is the data gathering stage of story crafting. Lack of clarity in what you want to say and why to say it is the number one reason that stories fail to serve their purpose.

Note: The Profile is not a story; it's a profile. It's your data. It's an aerial view of what you're selling.

The first profile you are going to create is your Product Profile. Though you may not be selling a product, from here on, I am going to use the word "Product" to make things simple. Translate Product to mean whatever you are "selling" to your audience. This is the information pertaining to the product you are selling—or the service—or the information, the message, the idea, the cause, or the lesson. The Product is your solution—your answer—the thing you are excited to be sharing with the world.

If you are in sales, you may think you have the Product Profile down to a science. Product knowledge is key to being able to sell a product effectively, but product knowledge is not the same thing as product story. Don't assume you have this covered. Play along. Story is the tool that gives your product knowledge meaning.

Speakers, you may struggle here. You may be have a lot to say, but lack focus and clarity on what your specific solution is. But we're not working on an entire speech; we are working on a story. Boil it down to one thing—one lesson you want to teach through that story—one point you want to make. You can cobble them together later.

Business owners, this story could be the story that sells your business to the world—your elevator pitch, your web copy, the story you tell at the local Rotary.

Non-profits, this could be your collective story—the one everybody in your organization or support circle shares in their own individual unique way to raise awareness.

Financial Planners, this could be a story that sells one aspect of your service—one particular thing your company does really well.

Politicians, this could be the story that shows people who you are and what you believe in.

Leaders, this could be the story of a solution you have to a problem the company is experiencing—or a vision story that you want to connect your employees to.

I leave it to you to apply The Story Formula™ to your own business, those you want to influence, and what you need them to do, think, or feel.

OVERVIEW

Product Profile: The product profile tells the story of the product you are selling to the world. It is the solution you have to a problem or a desire. It is the list of ingredients in your Healthy Cake. It is the ability to forgive in business. It is the way in which you want your people to start serving customers. Your profile includes the features of this new "healthy cake."

The Product Profile explains WHAT you created, what it DOES, and WHY it matters.

Example: Mr. Bean offered a detailed list of every ingredient included in and excluded from his cake, what benefits were offered, how much research had been put into its creation, and what it was able to do to address a certain problem or desired result.

NOTES

PRODUCT PROFILE WORKSHEET

Product Name _____

Fill out as many of these lines as you can. While they won't all end up in your final story, writing down the information will provide valuable intel when you create future stories.

$$w + y = pp$$

w	What it is/what it does
y	Why it matters to the world

What it is / What it does + Why It Matters   = pp

_____ _____ _____
_____ _____ _____
_____ _____ _____
_____ _____ _____
_____ _____ _____
_____ _____ _____
_____ _____ _____
_____ _____ _____
_____ _____ _____
_____ _____ _____
_____ _____ _____
_____ _____ _____
_____ _____ _____

NOTES

9
CREATE YOUR BUYER PROFILE

I once had a phone salesman talk for ten minutes about how he could help me with the merchant services for my design company before I could finally interrupt him and tell him he had the wrong number. I once saw a speaker make fun of someone their audience held in very high regard. I heard a salesman make a joke about liberals to a room full of liberals. I watched a speaker pull someone up from the audience to help them redesign their elevator pitch, only to find that the person was a secretary. In the world of comedy, if there is one sure way to fail, it's to not know your audience.

We don't sell the story of our product. We sell the story of what that product means to the person who will use it. There is a *big* difference.

The guy who sold me my iPad cover thought I was buying it for its functionality. He didn't know I bought it because I liked the color.

We don't buy for your reasons; we buy for *ours*.

We buy for emotional reasons: How we feel about you, how we feel about the product, and how we feel about ourselves wearing your solution.

If you are going to use story effectively as a tool, you need to know the person you are using it on. If you want to impact and influence, you need to understand what makes the person you want to impact tick. Too many people are so focused on what they want to say, without thinking of what their buyer needs to hear.

If your job is to show what that product means to your customer, you have to know what they want. Take time to research, think about, and document your Buyer.

Most of you have more than one buyer, motivated by more than one thing, which means one story isn't going to fit all.

Let me save you some time. Some of the things most people want overlap, and you'll probably have more to add about the person you are trying to influence. You'll get a chance to do that on the worksheet. This should give you a head start. Most people want:

- Security and Safety
- Shelter
- Food
- Clothing
- Love
- Belonging
- To be Courted (customer wants to know you want their business)
- To be Heard
- To be Acknowledged
- To be Remembered
- To be Financially Stable
- To be Rich
- To be a Rock Star
- To be Noticed
- To Have More Time
- To Work Less
- To be Happy / Content
- To be a Good Person

- To be Good Parents
- Happy Relationships
- Thin Thighs
- To Have Muscles
- To be Pretty
- To Live Longer
- To be Free From Pain
- To Have Control Over Their Life
- To be Respected in their Job
- To Win
- To be In The Spotlight
- To be Chosen
- To be Sexy
- To be Admired
- To be Smart
- To have a life partner

What *really* matters is what the person you want to influence wants. The more you are in touch with this, the more impact you will have.

When I speak to audiences about being the pink zebra, I talk about what it feels like to be weird—to be rejected—to have no group that claims me—and the desire to be accepted and validated. When I use those words—the words of how I feel in my pain and the desires I seek—I have the deepest level of connection with my listener who feels that same pain or desire.

We don't connect to someone else's plot; we connect to their emotion.

When your wound/desire mirrors that of your buyer and is *verbalized*—you have connection.

Feelings and emotions play a big part in strategic storytelling because we connect and buy based on how we feel—the pain of what we're feeling—or the feeling of wanting something desperately. When we as Sellers can mirror that pain/feeling to our audience, and they recognize their wound in ours, we have connection.

One of the biggest mistakes Sellers make is deciding what their customer wants. The key is to listen closely and just give them what they're asking for. Before you can do that, you have to know what they want.

The Buyer Profile is where you should spend most of your time and energy. You should always be in a constant state of answering these questions about your buyer. I use this buyer profile when I need to create a connection story with all sorts of groups like dairy farmers, six-year-olds, lunch ladies, senior citizen women, missionaries, national guard volunteers, etc. You can see just by looking at each of these different types of Buyer, that they are going to be motivated by different things. "Motivated" is the key word. Know what motivates your buyer.

Let's get to work. I recommend that you make a copy of the Buyer Profile before you write on it, so you'll have the template for future use.

BUYER PROFILE WORKSHEET

To connect and engage with your Buyer, you must know their story. Gather as many details as you can about your customer. You never know when that intel will prove useful for a story. Circle the questions about the Buyer that have a direct correlation to the product or to you. Feel free to add your own. Add comments on the following page.

**BUYER / ME = EVERYTHING I HAVE EXPERIENCED,
AM EXPERIENCING, WILL EXPERIENCE TOMORROW
AS IT RELATES TO YOUR PRODUCT**

What is happening in my life?

What happened yesterday?

What will happen tomorrow?

What makes me mad?

What makes me sad?

What do I want/need urgently?

What pain do I feel?

What lessons have I learned?

What are the resulting beliefs?

What do I value, cherish, and love?

What are my secret fantasies?

What are my deepest fears?

How do I want to be seen by others?

What mistakes have I made?

How do I view people like you?

What do I think about your product?

What genetic traits, personality do I have?

How do I see myself?

How do I see others?

What's my age?

What is my walk of life?

What is my history?

What are my wishes?

What are my regrets?

What makes me happy?

What does my day look like?

What do I wish my day would look like?

How do I feel about salespeople?

What is my history with your product?

What is my history with your company/brand?

How distracted am I?

How fast do I make decisions?

How confident am I?

How fulfilled am I at work?

How fulfilled am I at home?

How do other people at work treat me?

How do I feel about my superiors?

Who depends on me?

Who do I depend on?

Who do I trust and why?

Who do I not trust and why?

IDEAL BUYER
BUYER PROFILE (*bp*)

BUYER PROFILE COMMENTS

10
CREATE YOUR SELLER PROFILE

*I*t is important that you create your BUYER PROFILE before you create the SELLER PROFILE, as the details in your Buyer Profile will affect the details of your Seller profile.

The purpose of the Seller Profile is to gather the data and details that allow you to become the person they trust, like, believe, and feel like they know. This your chance to have them walk away with more than your information, but walk away with the meaning this information has to you personally. As I said earlier, sales is about emotional connection between Seller and Buyer. As a professional speaker, they buy me as much as they buy my advice.

I have a client who is the CEO of a healthcare organization. Her theme this year is Storytelling (more specifically, telling the patient story) and she wants the leaders of the hospital to develop strategic storytelling as a competency in their teams. They all took my online *Storytelling for Engagement Course* to develop their connection stories which will be used in a variety of ways throughout the hospital—from engaging employees, teaching, creating remarkable patient relationships, and marketing. Each one of these areas uses story in a different way to achieve a different result. In each case, we have a different buyer, a different product, and a different seller. The CEO herself had to tell the story of how Storytelling is a valuable competency and is worthy of their attention, despite their busy schedules. She hired me (now I have become the Seller) to come speak at her leadership summit, to motivate her people (my buyers) to embrace the power of story (our product.)

When the CEO is the seller of this product, she has already established some degree of trust between herself and her employees—or at least we'd like to think so. Maybe not, in which case, she still has the job as Seller to not just sell the product, but to make it personal. Why does this matter so much to her? When we can see the emotional attachment she has to the product, we are more likely to connect than if she just gave us the data. Motivation beats manipulation. Telling someone to do something is not as effective as making them *want* to do it.

When I was the speaker in her leadership summit, I became the Seller. I was a stranger. The audience didn't know me, trust me, believe me, or have a reason to like me. I couldn't jump straight to selling the data until I made it personal. I had to get them to uncross their arms and lean in, otherwise I'd be just another talking head adding more work to their day.

We embarked on a project to gather their stories. In some cases stories were used to encourage teams that their job mattered. Some stories put the employee into the shoes of the patient and reconnected them to the value in their work and the end result, even if they worked in a cubicle in the accounting department. Some stories were created to teach a difficult concept to a young doctor, or to explain to a patient what was going on inside their body. In every case, it was clear who was talking, who was listening, and what the story was intended to do, teach, or make someone feel.

Then it got a little trickier.

A group of people in the organization wanted to use the stories in marketing and branding—a great way to tell the story of their hospital. Data compels but the story sells. They knew they had to go beyond just telling people what they do. Story is not just what you do; it's who you are. It's data made personal. It's the Buyer becoming human—because patients don't do business with systems; they do business with people.

But how do you write a Seller profile when there are so many Sellers—when there isn't anybody talking to us? When they are just words on a page? When that story is going to be shared by many?

In this case, the Seller becomes a *we* and your task is to tell *our* story in way that makes *us* sound like people. We are the faces of your healthcare organization. We at Free Fitness have made it our mission…. We as part of the Research and Development team have dedicated ten years to this one specific area of research….

Side note: While it is helpful for healthcare organization to have a *We…* story, I also recommend that they not worry about having one *We…* story, but rather, a collection of individual stories printed on posters or in a catalog—each one telling the story of an individual. "I am the face of XYZ insurance, and I love my job because I get to help you in times of your greatest need."

There are a lot of moving pieces. The key is to be *very clear* on who the seller is for a given story, who the buyer is, and what the product is.

For every story you must choose specifically what it's intended to do (Product), who is selling it (Seller), and who you want to buy it (Buyer).

As I said earlier, we all want to influence someone, which makes us salespeople—and people buy from people they like, trust, believe, and feel they know—which is personal. Therefore, to truly have connection, you have to get personal with your buyer. They have to see you as more than a talking head. To buy from you, I have to feel like I know *you*. This is the purpose of creating your seller profile.

The Seller Profile establishes you as the *Trusted Source.* Only you can determine how much trust has already been established between the buyer and seller.

A quick note about brand stories: Many small business owners and professional speakers will spend a lot of time and energy writing their "brand story." Brand stories are important, but a brand story is not the story you choose to tell your customer. It's the story you want your customer to "write" about you based on the personal experience they had working with your brand. When I was a new speaker, I wrote the story of who I wanted to be. But over time, the story I wrote didn't match the story *they* wrote. What I intended to give them didn't match what they were actually receiving. That's when my brand story began to change to reflect more of what they were experiencing with me than what I told them to experience.

When I tell my professional speaker clients that they aren't connecting on stage, and need to get more personal with their audiences, they look at me confused. "I don't know what to tell them about myself."

"If you were going into a birthday party at your cousin's house, would you ask me what you should say to people inside? Probably not. You'll just go into the party and chat with people. Connecting as a Seller isn't too much different, except that you get to plan what you want to share. I just want to know something about you as a person; that will make you human to me."

Still not helpful? Don't worry. I've broken it down even more for you. I'll give you a series of questions to answer. But first let me explain one important component of your Seller Profile: Common Ground.

Your goal is twofold. Yes, you want to become personal, but in a way that makes you relatable to the buyer and their pain/desire/motives. Therefore, I want you to find things that you have in common with your buyer. This is easy because there are certain things we all have in common—or at least many of us do. Your answers might change based on your audience, where you live, the industry, etc.

When I want to connect with an audience, I tell jokes about or discuss details that are universal in our ability to relate to them:

1. **Relationships** (being married, divorced, dating, anniversaries, struggles that come in a relationship)
    a. Example: My husband and I just had a wedding anniversary. He gave me a dust buster. Yeah, apparently there's the gold anniversary, crystal, and dirt.
2. **Pets**
    a. Example: The things I love most in the world are my wife, my kid, and my dog—not necessarily in that order.)

3. **TV Shows**

    a. Example: I'm addicted to *CSI*. I've watched so many episodes that I'm pretty sure I could perform an autopsy if we needed one today—in heels.

4. **Kids**

    a. I have one son. He's precious. He's out in the car right now if you want to go take a peek

    b. Sports (I don't follow sports, so you're on your own on this one.)

5. **Others**

    a. Where you're from

    b. Personality Traits—the weird ones (OCD, addicted to office supplies)

    c. Hobbies (even if they don't share your hobby, it still makes you a little more human)

If you're standing on a stage giving a presentation or a sales pitch, you have a little more time to get personal. But when time is limited, there is one main goal: to tell us why your product works and why this it means so much to you personally.

This is your chance to connect the Product (Brand/Company) with your face and show us what it means to you to be part of this company and the solution you provide.

The *We...* story needs to be a collective story of who you all are in relation to the work you do and why it matters to you.

Your profile isn't really about what you've done; it's about who you are.

There are no hard and fast right or wrong answers, and there are many ways to get the result you seek.

We don't need to know your whole life history; that's too much information and too personal. In cases where time is limited, or the platform is on paper or the web, you might just have to limit the "you story" to the most important personal details—the ones that relate to the product and the buyer.

Find common ground between you, the product, and the buyer— things both of you experience and relate to.

Share feelings and emotions related to your own experience(s)—not just what you do but who you are and why this product is important to you. Choose personal profile details that mirror theirs.

SELLER PROFILE WORKSHEET

$$sp = s\ (cg)\ b$$

Seller Profile = Common Ground between Seller and Buyer

Explain not just what you do, but who you are. Why does this product matter to you personally? How does it make you feel?

Questions To Help You Write Your Seller Profile

1. Why do you care about this product (or idea)?

   _____
   _____

2. Why should we trust you?

   _____
   _____

3. Why should I believe you?

   _____
   _____

4. Why does this matter so much to you?

   _____
   _____

5. How can you relate to my pain?

   _____
   _____

6. How can you relate to the desire I have?

_____

_____

7. What do we have in common?

_____

_____

8. Who are you in relation to the Product you are here to sell?

_____

_____

11
PUTTING IT ALL TOGETHER
CRAFT YOUR CONNECTION STORY

*C*ongratulations. The heavy lifting is done. The most important stage of story crafting is gathering intel to write your story. Put it together to create your Connection Story *(cs)*.

Structure Your Details

Now that you have gathered your details, recap what you have.

$$w + y = pp$$

w	What it is/what it does
y	Why it matters to the world

bp = Buyer's Pain/Desire
As It Relates to Your Product

,

$$sp = s\ (cg)\ b$$

Seller Profile = Common Ground between Seller and Buyer

Put all the data together to create your *cs*—Connection Story.

$$bp + pp + sp = cs$$

You already have more details you need. You just stocked your pantry. You can write lots of cool stories with all this information about your product and your buyer, but we only want to make one thing right now—one story—to serve one specific purpose—to sell one thing to one buyer. This is your **Connection Story.**

You could probably find the details you need right now and plug them into the formula ($bp + pp + sp = cs$). Maybe you're already done. Have fun. We'll see you later. But if you're sitting there stumped, let's put this together in a way that makes sense.

We'll use my handy dandy Speech Structure System. You don't have to write a speech, (unless you want to. If you are a speaker, you can use this technique if you're struggling to define your core content.). Your Connection Story will follow the same concept.

My Speech Structure Template walks you through setting up your story to accomplish what you need to accomplish in a logical order. The Speech Structure answers some basic questions like:

Who am I?
Why am I here?
What is the problem we face?
How did I experience that problem
What solution do I have to offer?

The order can be rearranged as you see fit. Filling out the Speech Structure System Worksheet should be easy, since you can look at all the data you have already gathered to find your answers.

KELLY SWANSON'S CONTENT TEMPLATE FOR CREATING PRESENTATIONS

Who Am I?

Not what you've done or accomplished, but who you are. What makes you real, likable, a person others feel they know and can relate to?

People do business with people they like, trust, believe, and feel like they know. You are a sales person—connect first so you become a *person,* not a talking head. Don't brag. We don't care. It doesn't matter what you choose to tell us: where you're from, weird hobbies, which kid you were when you were growing up, shows you're addicted to. Pick things you might have in common with your audience.

_____

_____

_____

_____

_____

_____

What Do We Have in Common?

Standing on that stage, you are a mystery to your audience—untouchable—on a pedestal. Get down from "up there" and "get beside" them. Find common ground. Show them you can relate to their problems or goals. If you have nothing in common, tell them about someone you know/loved/were related to who shared their walk of life.

Example: I may not have anything in common with a room full of dairy farmers, but I can tell a story about a dairy farmer I once knew.

Example: I don't know anything about the insurance industry, but I know how much I value my own insurance and how important my rep is in my life.

People don't engage with us until they feel they have *connected* with us—until they feel like we "get them" and they can relate to us on some level.

Hint: Think of things we have universally in common—our kids learning to drive, being married, trying to pick a cough syrup at the drug store.

_____

_____

_____

_____

_____

Why Am I Here?

State your intent. "I am here to teach you three steps to improving productivity." This is as a short statement of what they will learn—kind of like repeating the program description. Sometimes I move this block to a later point in the program, but some people in the audience want to know where your presentation is going.

_____

_____

_____

_____

_____

The Goal(s) We Desire

All of us want the same thing(s)—to make money, sell more, deliver better customer service, be stronger leaders, etc. Don't just head to what they *say* they want. Head to what they *really* want. This may not be what their bosses want. What are they lying in bed at night asking for? Hit on all of it to improve the odds that they'll nod and say, *"Yes! I need that in my life."* This is far more effective than jumping straight to telling them what they need for them. Yuck.

_____

_____

_____

_____

_____

_____

What Stands in Our Way of Achieving This?
the problem we face

Here's where we get to the problem you are here to fix—or even one step above it. Sometimes what seems to be one problem has a different underlying problem. Don't overthink this. The objective here is to get your audience to nod and say, "Yes! I have that problem." or "Wow. I thought I had *that* problem, but it looks like I really have *this* problem." Sometimes you are here to solve *many* problems. Great. Offer more value to the audience.

Why?

_____

_____

_____

_____

_____

What Happens if We Don't Fix it?

_____

_____

_____

_____

_____

_____

What Happens if We Do?

_____

_____

_____

_____

_____

_____

Ask the audience: "Wouldn't *you* like to have this happen?" There's a psychological reason why it's good to have them nod and say, "yes." That's a subtle "buy in" from your audience.

Here's How I Experienced This Problem In My Life

Just like you, I had this same problem. Here is how it played out in my life:

_____

_____

_____

_____

_____

_____

_____

How I Fixed This Problem (First I Had To...)

Often our solutions to problems sit beneath a bigger umbrella solution that holds everything. Address this before you get to the three ways to fix it.

If I'm helping people improve sales, I will point out that the problem is that they're aren't selling effectively. Why? Because they are leaving out the most important step—connection. Connection is the new shift in perspective. Remember in *City Slickers* when the cowboy kept holding up his finger and saying, "It's all about this one thing?" Many speakers have that one thing at the core of their content. Don't overthink this if you don't have one umbrella solution or shift. It's perfectly okay to skip this part and go on to the next.

_____

_____

_____

_____

_____

Then I had to...

Here you can list three main points—answers to the problem. Three isn't a rule, but keynote speeches often have three main points. Audiences can't remember and connect to more than that.

1. _____

2. _____

3. _____

How much you explain under each point is up to you. You may have only a few sentences to say in that lesson, or you may have fifteen minutes of information to share. You may want to say more in number 1 than you do in number 3. It's all okay. These are your creative choices.

Note: Each main point can be broken down into its own formula if you have the time and like the model:

Share a Story —a case where this lesson applied to real life—Lesson + Action Step for the Audience

What Happened In My Life As a Result?

_____

_____

_____

_____

_____

_____

What happened to others when they followed my advice?

_____

_____

_____

_____

_____

I Know What You're Thinking!

This is your chance to handle the "yes-buts" that you know are going through their mind—their objections. "Yes, but you don't know my boss…."

_____

_____

_____

_____

_____

If I Can Do This, So Can You

Tell them how easy this is. With three little steps.

1. _____
2. _____
3. _____

Call To Action

This is where you get them to do what you want them to do: Sign up for something, access a gift, go to your Facebook page, buy your book, refer you, etc. Be careful of asking them to do too many things. Ask for too many and they'll choose none. Try to ask them to do only one thing.

_____
_____
_____
_____
_____

Questions and Answers

Optional. You can always have them ask questions in the hallway. No need to do it here.

_____
_____
_____
_____

Power Close

You need some sort of powerful way to close. Recap a point. End with a poem. Bring a story back around to completion. This doesn't really fall into the area of the content outline—I just want to make sure you don't end on Q&A—and make sure you know that your opening and closing need to be powerful.

_____

_____

_____

_____

_____

There you have it—a general template that will help you craft your keynote speeches. I use it all the time. The boxes don't have to stay in that order. And you certainly don't have to follow this template. Speeches are pieces of creative writing—you make all the decisions. But if structure is an issue for you, this will help you gather your thoughts in the first stage of the process.

Keep in mind that this template only deals with content—with *what you want to say.* It has nothing to do with *how you say it.* Stories and anecdotes and one-liners and humor and act-outs and everything else you add to this create be the true "magic sauce" that transforms your speech from data and content into connection, engagement, and show .

WRITE YOUR CONNECTION STORY

You have done a lot of work gathering information and creating a structure for your story, but at this point, it's not a story; it's just a series of facts and emotions. And here is where most people miss the mark. Let's talk about what a story is and what it isn't. (In this book, we are not talking about fiction; we are talking about strategic storytelling used in business to impact and influence.)

How Do We Define A Strategic Story?

A Strategic Story is a descriptive tale of a character with a conflict (pain or desire) that illustrates the conflict your listener is experiencing. It conveys the emotional pain that the main character experiences because of this conflict (Buyer recognizes pain and connects on an emotional leverl).

It sends the character on a journey to relieve this pain (buyer can relate).

The Character than meets the Buyer or Product who offers a solution.

The pain is resolved.

The character is transformed.

The character feels a sense of emotional victory (Buyer test drives—experiences—the solution).

A lesson is revealed (Buyer attaches his need to the solution offered by the seller).

Advice/Action Step given to listener.

Simple Version: A story is an example of someone with a problem who used your solution to achieve a positive outcome.

Take all those details you've put into a structure, and find a story that wraps it all up. Look for *parable* to wrap up that cold, shivering *naked truth* in. You've made your healthy cake, but you need a story to help you sell it.

12
HAPPILY EVER AFTER

*M*r. Bean's Baked Goods remained a reputable fixture of Prides Hollow for years, until the black awning faded to gray and the letter B wandered off the sign, leaving "Mr. Bean's aked Goods." I'm pretty sure nobody even noticed. His tiny shop bell rung daily for years with a steady stream of patrons until Mr. Bean grew old and gray and kept mixing up the sugar and salt—though people pretended not to notice. One evening Mr. Bean put the *Closed* sign on the door and never turned it back over.

When Mr. Bean died, everyone came to his service. People stayed late into the night sharing sugar-coated memories of Mr. Bean. Booker Diggs said he couldn't imagine spending another birthday without his gluten-free chocolate éclair. Ima Jean told the story of the time Mr. Bean drove three hours to deliver her daughter's wedding cake, making sure not to go above 20 miles an hour so he wouldn't mess it up. Old Widow Jenkins told the story of how every Sunday morning she would come in for a fresh blueberry muffin before church. When she broke her hip and couldn't go to church anymore, Mr. Bean delivered her muffin to her house. He even stayed and listened to the online sermon with her. Good man, that Mr. Bean. They all agreed.

Mr. Bean had learned how to sell his Healthy Cake from his mentor. He learned about building trust and rapport. He learned how to stop focusing on what he wanted to sell, and more on what his customers wanted to buy. He learned that everybody has a different story, and to be an influencer, he needed to find out what that story was. Mr. Bean became skilled at The Story Formula and was able to connect and engage with the people he served.

Mr. Bean made a *difference*. And that had very little to do with cake.

You can create profiles and formulas to map and chart your level of influence, but at the end of the day, connection isn't about a formula. It's about connecting to people. It's about finding meaning and purpose. It's why we're here. Story is the key.

Appendix I
STORYTELLING TIPS

How long should my story be?

That depends on whether you are telling the story or writing it—whether you're giving a presentation or creating a video—how much time or space you have. It's good practice to limit your stories to 5–10 minutes—about a page—or 3 to 4 paragraphs of about 500 words each.

Understand the Difference
Between the Written Word and the Spoken Word

Stories that are written to be read in a book are different than stories created to be told live. You cannot take a written story and assume it will sound good if you memorize it and tell it. Words are put together differently on a page intended for reading, than on a page intended to be spoken. Why? Because words on paper involve only one mode of communication. Only one person is involved—the reader. Telling the story out loud allows for the delivery style and any accompanying visuals to play a part in how the story feels. Spoken stories involve two (or more) people—a speaker and a listener.

When you sit down to "write a story," you might be in the wrong mode. Shift into "I'm going to sit down and write a *conversation*" mode. Keep reading and it will make more sense.

A Good Story Depends on Good Writing

Whether you script a story out, memorize it, and deliver it word for word, or not, when you pay attention to the words you choose, the story will be better than if you "wing it." Choose words that matter. Some words have more power than others. There's a beat and a timing to a story that will make it resonate. Cutting out clutter will increase its power. Taking the time to *craft* a good story is the first step.

Your story won't be as strong as it could be if it isn't planned out well. Great delivery can't make up for poorly written material with weak structure.

Don't Change Your Voice, Mannerisms, or Personality

The biggest mistake I see people make when telling a story, is that they become someone else. They take on a different voice. They make movements that aren't natural for them, or natural for the story. They "perform" the story instead of just telling it to me. If I don't believe that's the real you up there, I will disconnect. I don't want your happy Sunday school voice or the one you channel when you think of Shakespeare. I want you—the same way you would talk if you were sitting beside me on a plane (but without all the ums).

Practice telling your story the way you talk, using words you would normally use. Pause in the places where people often pause. Use movements that you would naturally use when telling that story—movements that support the story, not distract from it.

Tell Me What You're Thinking

One of the easiest and quickest ways to tell a story more naturally is to interject what you're thinking in the story as you tell it. Make your own commentary. You're allowed.

You can tell a story and have a conversation with us at the same time. Speeches are conversations, not performances.

> He named his first cake *Healthy Cake,* which didn't win him any awards for creativity, but that's what it was—a healthy cake. Just made sense. His wife would have been proud. It was too late for her, but Mr. Bean knew he could help others. Suddenly his work took on a lot more meaning.

The non-award-winning quality of Mr. Bean's product naming skills is not technically part of the story, but commenting on it adds a note of warmth and humor. It's more interesting than telling the story "straight."

Tell Me What I'm Thinking

You don't have to just address what you're thinking; you can address what you *think* I'm thinking. This isn't as tricky as it sounds. We do it all the time in natural conversation with our friends. We tell a certain part of a story, see the listener's reaction, and react to their reaction. We might say, "I know; sounds crazy, doesn't it?" It's how we dialogue naturally in real life.

You can do this when telling a story on-stage too. You don't even need an actual reaction from the audience if you can guess what they're thinking. Just assume somebody is thinking it, make eye contact with anyone, and say, "I know, right?" The audience will assume you are reacting to someone around them. Pretty cool.

> "I know what you're thinking: You're thinking there's no way it could have happened like this, but it did. And here's how I know...."

Be comfortable, present, and aware of your audience as you tell your story. Even when you're practicing it, picture your listener(s) sitting there. Stories involve two-way communication, even if the other person doesn't say a word.

Trip Over Your Words

Be okay with messing up your words. Pause to think of a word you want.

"She was over the top. No, that's not the right word. She was downright wacky."

When you do this, the audience knows you are one hundred percent in the moment. It's more believable. And that's when they connect. You can actually write this stuff into the story. You can *plan* to stumble over your words. Or you can be comfortable enough to mess yourself up a little on stage. Your listeners will know you're human and love you for it.

Step Into Your Story, Not Away From It

Many people tell stories like they're reading the phone book—like they are disconnected from the story. Don't step away and talk about it like you're discussing the weather. Go back into your story. Act it out. Share how you felt in those moments. Feel those moments again. You have to feel it every time you tell that story, and let your audience feel it too. If this sounds difficult, go back and write more descriptions and feelings into your story. The right words will cue you to invoke the proper delivery style.

What people didn't know about Mr. Bean was that he was a fresh widow. His wife had died from diabetes. In addition to <u>missing his best friend in the world</u>, Mr. Bean felt an <u>added pressure</u> because <u>he considered himself part of the reason she'd died</u>. He'd been doing some research, and as it turns out, sugar had played a big part in taking away the person he loved most in the world. Sugar—the prime ingredient on which Mr. Bean's livelihood was based. You can imagine.

Can you imagine how Mr. Bean is feeling? Would you tell a story like this in a monotone or would the descriptions help make your delivery sincere?

Don't Be Afraid of Silence

Your audience is several beats behind you. They are hearing your story for the first time. They are listening, processing, and then feeling the story. They need some time to get the joke. They need some time to see the details.

Stop when you make a point, end a sentence, or get to a meaningful or funny moment. It means you don't want to rush. The perfect way to slow yourself down is to force yourself to take a sip of water. This pause allows your listener to think through what you've just said.

Storytelling Tip: Don't Drop The Dog

As an award-winning storyteller, motivational speaker, and writer, I have spent my life studying the art and business of story—more specifically, how to write and tell a powerful story that increases your impact and influence. Every presentation/speech/story has two major components, each as important as the other—the script, and the delivery.

Stay In-scene

I was watching a speaker tell a story that involved a dog. He was acting out the story (which I strongly recommend) and the dog was a key player in the scene. The story was great and he did a good job telling it. I was hooked—until he dropped the dog—and then stepped on it! From that moment on, the poor squished dog was all I could think about.

As story crafters, if we do our jobs effectively, we paint the scene for our audience. As storytellers, our job is to stay in the scene. If you talking to your spouse in a story and speak to your left, don't come back a second later and continue the conversation facing right. If you are in the middle of a conversation that involves holding a dog, hold the dog throughout the conversation. Lack of consistency breaks the authenticity of the story because our brain receives conflicting data.

You don't have to act out every moment of your story, but for the parts that you do, be conscious of where you put people and objects in the scene. Hold to it. It's imaginary, but we can see everything.

Don't drop the dog.

A Quick Way To Create Colorful Characters

As a motivational speaker and comedian, stories are the key to my success, and characters are one secret to making listeners fall in love with your story. Many people who use stories in business tend to leave their characters flat. When we can't visualize a character, we can't relate to that character, and there goes your connection. Connection doesn't happen when we connect to the plot; it happens when we connect to a character in your story.

When you're crafting your story to be used as a tool of persuasion, don't neglect the people in it. Whether it's you or somebody else in the story, take the time to paint a picture of each character with a detail or two. We paint pictures of characters by describing what they look like, talking about their personalities, sharing their view of the world, how others view them, and what conflicts they face in their lives.

> Charlie O'Leary swears his knees don't hurt anymore since eating that cake. Ruth says she noticed a difference in her child's autism. Old Man Wiley says his cholesterol went down and he doesn't need to take medication anymore. Those are just a few of the stories that sell Mr. Bean's Healthy Cake.

These are minor characters in the Bean's Bakery story, but you can see that they're regular people who deal with aging and the aches and pains of life—just like we all do. A simple detail about painful knees or cholesterol or autism is the simple brushstroke that creates a portrait of each of them.

Use The Internet

In order to create these colorful characters, I decided to do a little Internet research. I searched "things old people to do" and landed on lots of chat pages where this subject came up and people wrote in their answers. I cut and pasted them into a list that I use to create characters. At this point, I already have 75 traits on my list. Here are some of the things on my list:

- They leave their turn signals on all day
- They drive 20 in a 60 mph zone.
- They complain about the room temperature and the music being too loud
- They suck on their dentures
- They don't go out to eat without a coupon
- They wear elastic waistband jeans with pockets
- They clip out newspaper articles and mail them to you
- They call you to ask you how to rewind the DVD player

Adding little details will bring a character to life, and (as an added bonus) make your listeners laugh. The items above are funny, not because they are jokes, but because we can relate to them. You *know* someone who does this.

How I Paint the Scene in a Story

A key to a compelling story is the details you choose. It almost doesn't matter what details you pick, as long as you take the time to paint a vivid picture. Your story becomes even more flavorful when you choose details that aren't obvious or predictable, and when you choose details that evoke an emotion or a memory.

Another way to bring the scene to life is by inserting your own emotion or memory, as the one taking in the scene. The vivid description can be in your own interpretation of the scene you are standing in.

While working on a story set at a small town parade, I looked for a few details that would paint the picture in a compelling way. I try to channel my inner Norman Rockwell. His paintings have always symbolized the town in which all my stories take place—Prides Hollow. Norman Rockwell was able to tell so many stories and bring out so many emotions and memories with one picture. You can do the same with words.

Use all your senses when describing a scene. What do you smell? What do you hear? What do you touch? What do you taste? How does this moment make you feel?

Don't just tell a story; tell how you are feeling in the moments of your story.

My memory of a small town parade had grown fuzzy over time, so I went on Google and typed in "small town parade images.". This was enough to jog my memory. If you are describing a scene and having trouble, find an image of a similar scene to help you pull out the details.

When I'm working on a story or a scene, I don't start writing; I make a list of bullet points. I don't worry about how to get into it or out of it. I'm just concerned with describing the details. Often when I get through, there really is no need to write out the scene of the story, I can just tell the details I have written down.

Here is what I came up with. I only need a few, so narrowing it down will be difficult. I will also change the order of the details so that they are told in the order that I would see them in a parade—just to make it easier to remember what comes first, and have a little chronological order to the details.

- There's an old guy in a rusty lawn chair sitting on the curb, waving a tiny flag—his cheek bulging from the tobacco his wife finally stopped nagging him about. He's wearing a jacket bearing the symbols of his service—which in Prides Hollow will still get you a nod of respect and a never ending chain of requests to hear the story of how he got that scar on his leg.

- The Queen of Potted Meat sits tall in the middle of a carnation-adorned float made out of tissue paper and streamers. She waves slightly to the crowds with a gentle nod of her head, so as not to disrupt the updo that had taken a team of chirping women all morning to spray in place. She's surrounded by her court of runners up—all wearing badges that will hang forever around their necks as a tribute to the good old days.

- The smells of fried funnel cakes and cotton candy blends in with the fresh hay that lines the flatbed of Hershel's truck carrying Maybelle—his blue ribbon pig from the state fair. Somehow the smell of manure and cotton candy mix just fine.

- Local politicians with canned smiles throw cheap candy out of restored cars—using this as an opportunity for exposure in a town that knew their daddy and their daddy's daddy—while mammas bellowed to their children to "get that last piece, Junior! Go get it!" with little thought of the danger involved with ordering their children to dodge tires and marching feet to catch a wayward tootsie roll.

- The flushed faces of the Boy Scouts pass by with their crooked bandanas and shirts that refused to stay tucked—whose freckles shiver excitedly because they are finally old enough to march (and Lord help us if Nathan's pocket holds another bullfrog like last year. This almost proved to be the death of a group of dainty young cloggers who were not expecting a frog to land on their shoulder in the middle of Foggy Mountain Breakdown). "He's doing it because he likes you," whispered his mother as she prayed her child would not start dating any time soon.

- The far away steady beat of the high school marching band drums heralds the arrival of the only instrument guaranteed to hit the right note all day. It's the heartbeat of a smalltown parade.

- A little girl dances in her bare feet just outside her parents' circle of view—twirling in her ballerina skirt and mismatched sequined tank top that does nothing to stop her self-appointed solo. She dances like nobody is watching—which is pretty accurate—in a moment of true unabashed joy that can only come with being five—and slips too quickly away as she wishes to be six.

The smalltown parade—that cherished tradition held on to way past the memory of why it existed. Perhaps it allowed people to stop what they were doing and grab a seat at the curb to smile at a neighbor and check in with a loved one? A smalltown parade froze all that was important into memory—right there on that street—wrapped in a fog of spun sugar and manure—a memory that will forever hang as a banner of the good old days.

Can you see it? Yeah. Me too.

Appendix II
WHAT WE ALL WANT

I once served on a vision casting committee at my church. The church had a long history in the community. I think Moses was a charter member. The church had good people with good hearts. But it was a dying church—literally. The congregation had grown older and never attracted younger people. It was facing extinction. Hence the reason for the forming of a vision casting committee to help save the church.

Six of us gathered in a quiet meeting room to solve a problem that was bigger than we were. It wasn't a matter of *having* new ideas. The problem was getting the congregation to *accept* new ideas. They were pretty set in their ways. They were more than willing to make changes, as long as we kept things the way they'd been for a hundred years.

What was even tougher was that these were our elders, strong contributors to the church, and part of its rich history. One wrong move and they would leave—or get rid of us.

We were smart enough to know that standing in front of the congregation and telling them what they needed to do, was not going to work. Trust me. We had tried it. We needed something to uncross their arms, lower their guard, and make an emotional appeal to inspire them to get behind our new ideas and this new vision.

Have you found yourself in a position of trying to convince someone to do something? It's not always easy is it?

What do we all want?

We want to influence someone so they do what we tell them to. We're all in the business of persuasion. This makes us all sales people—selling something and needing buy-in.

Problem? What's keeping us from getting that?

Telling them what to do is one thing. Getting them to do it, is another. Making them *want* to do it, is something else entirely. This can be quite the daunting task. It's not as simple as just telling them what to do.

What's keeping us from having maximum influence?

"All things being equal people will do business with, and refer business to, those people they know, like, and trust."

— *The Go-Giver* by Bob Burg and John David Mann

It has been estimated that 80 per cent of all buying decisions are based on emotion. The key to successful sales is making the right connection with the customer and extracting the right emotional response.
—*Emotional Selling: Using Emotional Intelligence to Get Sales* by David Yule

63 percent of people interviewed believe that in dealing with "most people" you "can't be too careful" and 37 percent believed that "most people would try to take advantage of you if they got a chance." Respondents also revealed that of the people that they "know personally" they would expect 85 percent of them to be fair."
—*New York Times/CBS News* poll, July, 1999

"People don't remember what you made them think, but they never forget how you made them feel."

—Maya Angelou

In my own research on stage, I learned the same thing: People don't remember what you made them think as much as they remember how you made them *feel*—about themselves—about you—and about the message you're sharing.

This is the mistake most of us make. We focus on data instead of on connection and emotion. We focus on the *what it is* instead of *what it means* and *why it matters*. So how do we go deeper into this art of connection to develop trust?

One Word: STORY.

Remember the Trojan Horse Story?

The Trojan Horse is a story from the Trojan war when the Greeks, facing a losing battle, decided to use their brains instead of their brawn. They crafted a giant wooden horse as a "gift" for the Trojans. Once the Greeks delivered the gift, they sailed off while the Trojans pulled the horse into the city as a trophy. But the horse wasn't just a horse; it was filled with Greek soldiers who surprised the Trojans and destroyed the city of Troy, ending the war. This is where we get the expression "Trojan Horse" which refers to the strategy of finding a subtle way into your opponent's safe place.

The Battlefield of Persuasion

While influencing others isn't a battle, we are still trying to get into the mind and heart of our listener, where true impact takes place. To influence is to win them over to our way of thinking.

But the battle of persuasion isn't won by force. True impact happens when you can find a way into their safe place, past the barriers that stand in the way of entry.

Strategic storytelling is the Trojan Horse of persuasion. Your facts can't get you into your opponent's safe place. To get past the barrier, you have to present those facts as a gift. This gift isn't a nice manicure set with your company logo imprinted on it. This gift is the story of *what they want.* This gift is the story of how your information applies to *their* life—how it eases *their* pain or helps them achieve *their* desire.

Once you have entered into your opponent's safe place (the heart of persuasion), you can share your information. And, who knows, maybe you'll never even need to pull out your sword!

> *PowerPoint presentations may be powered by state-of-the-art technology. But reams of data rarely engage people to move them to action. Stories, on the other hand, are state-of-the-heart technology—they connect us to others. They provide emotional transportation, moving people to take action on your cause because they can very quickly come to psychologically identify with the characters in a narrative or share an experience—courtesy of the images evoked in the telling.*
>
> —Peter Guber, *Psychology Today*

Telling stories is the best way to teach, persuade, and even understand ourselves.

> *All choices are ultimately personal choices and if you want to influence people's choices you will find that the most powerful form of influence is always personal.*
>
> —Annette Simmons, *The Story Factor*

Data is not personal. Stories are.

> *The ability to display images internally and order those images in a process is called thought." In other words, the thought processes of the mind work in association with the images we store at the cellular level.*
>
> —Antonio Damasio, Director of the Brain and Creativity Institute
> at the University of Southern California in *The Healing Code*
> by Dr. Alexander Lloyd and Dr. Ben Johnson

Those images, by the way, are a universal language. When we don't speak the language of another country, we usually resort to symbols to get our point across. This reinforces the fact that all people, no matter what language they speak, store data from their life experiences as a collection of images.

So, for our data to make sense—to be taught, to be stored, accessed in the mind of our listener—it must be wrapped in an image.

I have seen it happen for years in my career on a stage. If I stood on a stage and just told them what they needed to know, my career would be short-lived. It's the story I wrap it in that opens the heart and wraps the truth in an image they can step into, experience, and draw their own conclusions from.

The next time you find yourself in a position of influence, take a look at your data and find an example of how that data applies to real life. Story is simply the specific example of a person with a conflict that is resolved through your solution.

Story is your Trojan Horse.

Anyway … back to the church vision casting committee. We had tried everything, and finally all eyes turned to me. "You're the speaker; do something," they said.

But I wasn't a speaker back then; I was just a storyteller. What did I know? I could tell a good story. I could make people laugh and cry. But could I actually change their minds through story?

We had run out of options. They sent me off to write. And that morning instead of the sermon, they put me up there on that pulpit to "tell a story."

I told the story of a smalltown church that had burned down. They had lost everything material and traditional that symbolized their church. They had no choice but to hold Sunday service in a parking lot.

I told the story of how the people learned that church was more than a building—that church could be just as precious without a piano or pews, and that sometimes the collection was even bigger when nobody passed around a plate. I told of how the people learned that maybe what they thought mattered wasn't as important, after all. And this time, when they built the new church, it looked totally different. The congregation drew in hundreds of people who had heard their story.

As I told the story, I could see heads nodding in agreement. I watched the people in my audience step into my story and experience the truths there—without anger—without crossed arms or stubborn expressions.

I had found a way in.

At the end of the service, an elderly gentleman came up and pulled me aside. "You know," he whispered, "If you really think about it, that church was a lot like ours!"

You don't say.

From that point on, we had full cooperation from the congregation to move forward with our new vision.

If you think about it, maybe our dilemma at that little old church is a lot like the dilemma you're facing in your own life.

Maybe story is your way in.